VALENTINA HARRIS

Suppers

Photography by SIMON WHEELER

THE MASTER CHEFS

TED SMART

Valentina

VALENTINA HARRIS grew up in Rome, where she gained diplomas in teaching and cooking at the Scuola di Alta Cucina Cordon Bleu School. She moved to London in 1976.

In 1984 Valentina published her first cookery book, *Perfect Pasta*, which has since been translated into six languages. She has written a further 12 books, including *Recipes from an Italian Farmhouse* (1989), *Valentina's Complete Italian Cookery Course* (1992) and *Valentina's Italian Regional Cookery*, which accompanied a BBC-TV series of the same name.

Valentina regularly appears on television and radio, and contributes articles on various aspects of Italian cuisine to many newspapers and magazines. She is in great demand at food events and has given innumerable cookery demonstrations throughout Europe, in Australia, New Zealand, America and Japan.

CONTENTS

In Italy we

do not eat

to live, we

live to eat!

ALVARO MACCIONI, OWNER,

LA FAMIGLIA, LONDON

INTRODUCTION

I have always believed that food must feed much more than just the body. Real food feeds the soul too. Perhaps it is the Italian half of me that always makes me feel so emotional about food, but in cooking for so many people over the years, I am certain that we eat different things according to the mood we are in when we sit down to enjoy a meal.

Supper has a mood all of its own. It has none of the panic factor of a dinner party; we can invite people to supper and know that their expectations will somehow not be as high, even though the food will be delicious. There is a relaxed, easy-going feeling about supper, mixed up with a marvellous sense of comfort. For me, an ideal supper dish is one which requires minimal last minute preparation, which satisfies the appetite with one dish, and which more often than not can be cooked in the oven and served straight from the dish. I hope you will enjoy this collection of old favourites, which are all reminiscent of many happy suppers.

Valentina

BAKED FENNEL SOUP

6 LARGE FENNEL BULBS, OR
    8 SMALLER ONES, WASHED AND
    CUT INTO THIN SECTIONS,
    DISCARDING THE HARD
    EXTERIOR PARTS
100 G/3½ OZ UNSALTED BUTTER
SALT AND FRESHLY GROUND BLACK
    PEPPER
200 G/7 OZ FRESH, SOFT CHEESE
    (BEL PAESE, CAMEMBERT, BRIE),
    SLICED
9 SLICES OF CIABATTA BREAD,
    CUBED
2 TABLESPOONS FRESHLY GRATED
    PARMESAN CHEESE

SERVES 4

Preheat the oven to 160°C/325°F/
Gas Mark 3.

Boil the fennel in enough salted
water to cover, until tender. Drain,
reserving the liquid. Thoroughly
butter a large ovenproof dish and
arrange half the fennel in the dish.
Season lightly, then scatter half the
cheese over the fennel.

Fry the cubes of bread in half
the remaining butter, until golden.
Sprinkle half the fried bread cubes
over the fennel and cheese. Top
with another layer of fennel, salt
and pepper, cheese and bread
cubes. Pour the reserved liquid
over the top. Leave to settle for a
few minutes, then sprinkle with
the Parmesan and dot with the
remaining butter. Bake for about
35 minutes. Serve piping hot.

I like to follow this soup with a
platter of different kinds of salami
served with two or three types of
bread, and then a tray of oven-
baked apples.

RICE AND PEA SOUP

2 TABLESPOONS UNSALTED BUTTER

2 TABLESPOONS EXTRA VIRGIN
OLIVE OIL

2 ONIONS, CHOPPED

2 STICKS OF CELERY, CHOPPED

450 G/1 LB FRESH PEAS, SHELLED
WEIGHT, OR FROZEN PETITS POIS

300 G/11 OZ RISOTTO OR
PUDDING RICE

1 LITRE/1¾ PINTS CHICKEN OR
VEGETABLE STOCK (PAGE 30),
KEPT HOT

SALT AND FRESHLY GROUND BLACK
PEPPER

4 TABLESPOONS DOUBLE CREAM

8 TABLESPOONS FRESHLY GRATED
PARMESAN CHEESE

SERVES 4–6

Heat the butter and oil in a wide
saucepan, add the onions, celery
and peas and fry gently until the
onions are completely soft.

Add the rice and stir over
medium heat, adding the stock
little by little as the rice cooks and
absorbs the liquid. Continue to stir
and add liquid gradually, keeping
the texture very wet and soupy.
After about 10 minutes, season
with salt and pepper.

As soon as the rice is tender,
about 20 minutes, remove the pan
from the heat and stir in the cream
and the Parmesan. Serve at once.

Follow this soup-cum-risotto
with a platter of different kinds of
cheeses and a tomato salad.

HEARTY MUSSEL SOUP

1.5 KG/3 LB FRESH, LIVE MUSSELS,
   CLEANED (PAGE 28)
2–3 GARLIC CLOVES, LIGHTLY
   CRUSHED
4 TABLESPOONS EXTRA VIRGIN
   OLIVE OIL
HANDFUL OF CHOPPED FRESH
   FLAT-LEAF PARSLEY
2 TABLESPOONS PASSATA
SALT AND FRESHLY GROUND BLACK
   PEPPER
2 GLASSES OF DRY WHITE WINE
8 SLICES OF CIABATTA BREAD,
   LIGHTLY TOASTED AND RUBBED
   WITH A HALVED GARLIC CLOVE
OLIVE OIL TO DRIZZLE

SERVES 4

Put all the mussels into a large, wide saucepan with no extra liquid and place over a medium heat. Cover with a lid and shake the pan to help the heat get to all the mussels so they open. Once they are all open, take them out of the pan and strain their liquid. Reserve the liquid, discard all the mussels which remain closed and set the rest aside until required.

In the same pan, fry the garlic in the oil for about 5 minutes. Add the parsley and passata, season and stir well. Add the mussels and the wine and mix thoroughly. Cook over a high heat for about 4 minutes, then remove from the heat.

Arrange the toasted, garlicky bread in a wide bowl. Drizzle a thin stream of olive oil over the bread slices, then pour the mussel soup over the bread. Serve immediately, remembering to place an empty bowl in the middle of the table to collect empty shells.

Serve with plenty of ice-cold dry white wine.

CAULIFLOWER AND RICE BAKE

1 CAULIFLOWER, BROKEN INTO
    FLORETS
8 HEAPED TABLESPOONS RISOTTO
    RICE
1 ONION, THINLY SLICED
85 G/3 OZ UNSALTED BUTTER
4 TABLESPOONS DRIED WHITE
    BREADCRUMBS
SALT AND FRESHLY GROUND PEPPER
6 HEAPED TABLESPOONS FRESHLY
    GRATED PARMESAN CHEESE
1 LITRE/1¾ PINTS BÉCHAMEL SAUCE
    (PAGE 29)

TOMATO AND OLIVE SAUCE

2 GARLIC CLOVES, CHOPPED
4 TABLESPOONS OLIVE OIL
2 TABLESPOONS FINELY CHOPPED
    CAPERS
2 TABLESPOONS FINELY CHOPPED
    BLACK OLIVES
500 ML/16 FL OZ PASSATA
LARGE PINCH OF DRIED OREGANO

SERVES 4

Preheat the oven to 230°C/450°F/
Gas Mark 8. Steam the cauliflower
florets until only just tender, about
10 minutes.

Boil the rice in salted water for
10 minutes, then drain. Fry the

onion gently in half the butter in a
large, wide frying pan. Add the
partly cooked rice and mix
together for about 3 minutes, using
two forks in order to keep the rice
grains separate.

Thoroughly butter an
ovenproof dish and sprinkle with
breadcrumbs. Arrange half the
cauliflower in the dish, season
lightly, then cover with half the
rice, half the Parmesan and half the
béchamel sauce. Repeat the layers
and sprinkle the remaining
breadcrumbs on top. Dot with the
remaining butter and bake for
15–20 minutes.

Meanwhile, make the sauce; fry
the garlic in the oil for 5 minutes.
Add the capers and olives and fry
for a further 5 minutes. Add the
passata, simmer for about 10
minutes, then add the oregano and
season to taste. Keep warm until
ready to serve with the bake.

Serve with a leafy green salad
containing plenty of spicy-tasting
rocket (arugula).

BAKED STUFFED TOMATOES
with Italian sausage

6 LARGE, FIRM, ROUND BEEFSTEAK
   TOMATOES
200 G/7 OZ LONG-GRAIN OR
   RISOTTO RICE
2 GARLIC CLOVES, LIGHTLY
   CRUSHED IN THEIR SKINS
6–7 TABLESPOONS EXTRA VIRGIN
   OLIVE OIL
2 ONIONS, CHOPPED
200 G/7 OZ FRESH ITALIAN
   SAUSAGE, PEELED AND
   CRUMBLED, OR MINCED PORK
A FEW LEAVES OF FRESH BASIL
LARGE PINCH OF DRIED THYME
SALT AND FRESHLY GROUND BLACK
   PEPPER
¼ TEASPOON BEEF EXTRACT,
   DILUTED IN 125 ML/4 FL OZ
   HOT WATER
HANDFUL OF FRESHLY GRATED
   PARMESAN CHEESE

SERVES 4

Preheat the oven to 200°C/400°F/
Gas Mark 6. Cut the tops off the
tomatoes and scoop out the seeds
and cores. Turn them upside down
to drain for 30 minutes. Boil the
rice in plenty of salted water until
just tender. Drain and set aside.

Fry the garlic in 4 tablespoons
of the oil until browned, then
discard. Add the onions and fry
until soft, then add the sausage or
minced pork and stir thoroughly.
Add the basil and thyme and
season lightly. Simmer until the
meat is cooked through, adding a
little water or stock occasionally to
prevent it from drying out.

When the meat is thoroughly
cooked, mix it with the rice and
use to fill the tomatoes. Pour the
diluted beef extract into a baking
dish and arrange the tomatoes in
the dish. Sprinkle with olive oil
and plenty of grated Parmesan.
Bake for 30 minutes. Serve warm.

A salad of boiled green beans or
lightly boiled chard dressed with
lemon juice and olive oil is ideal
with this dish.

BAKED HERRINGS
with potatoes and button onions

1 KG/2¼ LB FRESH HERRINGS,
   HEADS AND SPINES REMOVED
300 G/11 OZ POTATOES
250 G/9 OZ BUTTON ONIONS,
   PEELED
85 G/3 OZ UNSALTED BUTTER
FRESHLY GROUND BLACK PEPPER
HANDFUL OF CAPERS PRESERVED
   IN SALT
FRESH FLAT–LEAF PARSLEY, CHOPPED

SERVES 4

Preheat the oven to 180°C/350°C/ Gas Mark 4. Clean the herrings very thoroughly. Slice the potatoes thickly. If the onions are larger than a walnut, cut them in half. Put 1 tablespoon butter in a frying pan and add the onions. Sauté the onions for about 5 minutes to soften them slightly.

Generously butter a large ovenproof dish and lay the herrings in the dish with the potatoes and onions. Season with pepper. Bake for about 10 minutes, then add the capers and parsley and continue cooking, basting frequently with the butter from the dish, for about 1 hour or until the potatoes are tender. Serve piping hot.

I like to serve this with a simple, really crunchy coleslaw salad, with a little wholegrain mustard added to the dressing.

SPINACH AND TOMATO LASAGNE

400 G/14 OZ LASAGNE SHEETS
1 KG/2¼ LB FRESH SPINACH OR
    500 G/1 LB 2 OZ FROZEN LEAF
    SPINACH
4 TABLESPOONS EXTRA VIRGIN
    OLIVE OIL
2 GARLIC CLOVES, CHOPPED
500 ML/16 FL OZ PASSATA
1 TABLESPOON CHOPPED FRESH
    FLAT-LEAF PARSLEY
SALT AND FRESHLY GROUND BLACK
    PEPPER
2 TABLESPOONS MELTED BUTTER
BÉCHAMEL SAUCE (PAGE 29)
250 G/9 OZ MOZZARELLA CHEESE,
    CUBED
150 G/5 OZ PARMESAN CHEESE,
    GRATED

SERVES 4-6

Bring a large saucepan of salted water to the boil. Cook the lasagne sheets four or five at a time, making sure they don't stick together. As soon as they are tender, remove them from the water and lay them on damp, clean tea towels, without touching, while you cook the remaining lasagne.

Cook the spinach in a little boiling water until just wilted, cool under running water, drain and squeeze dry.

Heat the olive oil in a saucepan, add the garlic and fry gently for about 5 minutes, then add the passata. Stir, then simmer for about 15 minutes. Add the parsley and seasoning and set aside.

Preheat the oven to 180°C/350°F/Gas Mark 4.

Brush an ovenproof dish with the melted butter. Pour a little béchamel sauce in the bottom of the dish and arrange a layer of lasagne sheets on top, slightly overlapping. Scatter over some spinach, mozzarella and Parmesan. Cover with the tomato sauce, then another layer of lasagne sheets.

Repeat the layers until all the ingredients have been used up, ending with a layer of béchamel sauce over the tomato sauce. Bake for about 45 minutes or until bubbling and lightly browned.

Serve with a salad of baby spinach and lambs' lettuce, dressed with a little balsamic vinegar and extra virgin olive oil, and plenty of bread or warmed focaccia for mopping up extra sauce.

COURGETTE AND CHEESE GRATIN

5 LARGE COURGETTES, TOPPED,
   TAILED AND WASHED
4 TABLESPOONS EXTRA VIRGIN
   OLIVE OIL
1 LARGE RED ONION, THINLY
   SLICED
5 FRESH EGGS, BEATEN
   THOROUGHLY
6 TABLESPOONS FRESHLY GRATED
   PARMESAN CHEESE
150 G/5 OZ MOZZARELLA CHEESE,
   CUT INTO SMALL CUBES
2 TABLESPOONS CHOPPED FRESH
   FLAT-LEAF PARSLEY
SALT AND FRESHLY GROUND BLACK
   PEPPER
3 TABLESPOONS DRIED WHITE
   BREADCRUMBS

SERVES 4–6

Preheat the oven to 180°C/350°F/
Gas Mark 4.

Cut the courgettes into cubes.
Heat the oil in a frying pan, add
the onion and fry until soft. Add
the courgette cubes and fry gently
until softened, turning frequently.

Oil an ovenproof dish large
enough to hold all the ingredients
with space at the top. Scatter a
layer of the courgette and onion
mixture in the dish. Cover with a
thin layer of eggs and sprinkle with
Parmesan, mozzarella and a little
parsley; season with salt and
pepper. Repeat until all the
ingredients have been layered in
the dish. Make sure the top is
covered with beaten egg. Sprinkle
the breadcrumbs on the top and
bake for about 30 minutes or until
well browned and crisp.

Serve with crusty bread and a crisp
green salad. Some torn basil leaves
are a good addition to the salad,
since the flavour of basil goes very
well with courgettes.

POLENTA PASTICCIATA

300 G/11 OZ YELLOW POLENTA
   FLOUR
SALT
4 TABLESPOONS OLIVE OIL
2 ONIONS, FINELY CHOPPED
1 GARLIC CLOVE, FINELY CHOPPED
1 STICK OF CELERY, CHOPPED
1 CARROT, CHOPPED
50 G/2 OZ PANCETTA, CHOPPED
500 ML/16 FL OZ PASSATA
1 BAY LEAF
SALT AND FRESHLY GROUND BLACK
   PEPPER
300 G/11 OZ MOZZARELLA
   CHEESE, CUBED
200 G/7 OZ PARMESAN CHEESE,
   GRATED
3 TABLESPOONS EXTRA VIRGIN
   OLIVE OIL

SERVES 6

Bring 2 litres/3½ pints water to the boil, add two pinches of salt and then rain the polenta into the boiling water, whisking vigorously. As soon as the polenta begins to thicken, take a large wooden spoon and stir constantly until the polenta comes away from the sides of the pan: this will take 50 minutes. Turn the cooked polenta on to a wooden board and leave until cold. This can be made the day before. Cut the cold polenta into strips about 8 cm/3 inches wide.

Heat the oil in a saucepan and fry the onions, garlic, celery, carrot and pancetta until the vegetables are soft. Add the passata and the bay leaf. Season, cover and simmer gently for about 45 minutes.

Preheat the oven to 190°C/375°F/Gas Mark 5.

Oil an ovenproof dish and arrange a layer of polenta on the bottom. Cover with a thin layer of the tomato sauce, then sprinkle with mozzarella and Parmesan. Drizzle with a little oil, then repeat the layers until all the sauce and cheese have been used up.

Bake the polenta for about 30 minutes. Serve piping hot.

If you have some polenta left over, grill it and drizzle it with a little oil. You can eat this while you wait for the main dish.

This is a very filling dish, so to follow I would recommend nothing more than a little salad and fruit, preferably some refreshing citrus fruit.

SQUID AND MUSHROOM STEW

1.8 KG/4 LB SQUID, CLEANED
   (PAGE 28)
4 TABLESPOONS EXTRA VIRGIN
   OLIVE OIL
3 GARLIC CLOVES, THINLY SLICED
300 ML/½ PINT FISH STOCK
   (PAGE 29)
1 LARGE GLASS OF DRY WHITE WINE
50 G/2 OZ DRIED PORCINI
   MUSHROOMS, SOAKED FOR
   30 MINUTES IN WARM WATER
SALT AND FRESHLY GROUND BLACK
   PEPPER
2 TABLESPOONS CHOPPED FRESH
   FLAT-LEAF PARSLEY

SERVES 4

Cut the squid into finger-sized strips. Heat the oil and garlic in a large saucepan over a low heat for about 6 minutes, then add the squid. As soon as the squid is heated through, add the stock and the wine. Cover and simmer gently for about 1 hour or until the squid is tender.

Drain the mushrooms carefully. Strain their soaking liquid and reserve. Chop the mushrooms and add them to the squid, then add the strained liquid. Season with salt and pepper. Simmer, uncovered, for a further 20 minutes.

Pour the stew into a large bowl, sprinkle with parsley and serve with mashed potatoes or creamy soft polenta.

THE BASICS

TECHNIQUES

CLEANING MUSSELS

Scrape off any barnacles and scrub the mussel shells. Pull out the 'beards' and discard, then rinse the mussels in plenty of cold water. Discard any mussels with broken shells and any that remain open.

CLEANING SQUID

Pull off and discard the head and tentacles; the clear, plastic-like backbone should come away at the same time, but run a finger inside the body sack to clean it out. Remove the purplish skin from the outside, then wash the squid thoroughly under running water.

BÉCHAMEL SAUCE

50 G/2 OZ BUTTER
50 G/2 OZ PLAIN WHITE FLOUR
500 ML/16 FL OZ MILK
SALT AND FRESHLY GROUND PEPPER

MAKES 500 ML/16 FL OZ
Melt the butter in a saucepan until
foaming, then stir in the flour until
a thick paste is formed. Pour in all
the milk and whisk vigorously to
prevent lumps from forming.
Simmer gently until thickened and
no flavour of raw flour can be
tasted in the sauce. Season to taste.

FISH STOCK

1 KG/2¼ LB WHITE FISH BONES
1 ONION, CHOPPED
1 STICK OF CELERY, CHOPPED
2 CARROTS, CHOPPED
1 SPRIG OF THYME

**MAKES ABOUT 1.2 LITRES/
2 PINTS**
Place the fish bones in a large
saucepan with 2.3 litres/4 pints
water, bring to the boil and simmer
very gently for 20 minutes. Strain
through a muslin-lined sieve into a
clean pan, add the vegetables and
thyme and bring back to the boil.
Simmer for 35 minutes, until
reduced to about 1.2 litres/2 pints.
Strain and season to taste.

CHICKEN STOCK

675 G/1½ LB CHICKEN WINGS, OR 1
   CHICKEN CARCASS
1 LARGE ONION, QUARTERED
2 LEEKS, ROUGHLY CHOPPED
2 CARROTS, ROUGHLY CHOPPED
2 STICKS OF CELERY, ROUGHLY
   CHOPPED
1 BAY LEAF
12 BLACK PEPPERCORNS

**MAKES ABOUT 900 ML/
1½ PINTS**
Place all the ingredients in a large
saucepan. Add 1 litre/1¾ pints
water. Bring slowly to the boil,
then simmer for 3 hours. Strain and
cool, then chill overnight.

   The next day, remove all fat
from the surface.

VEGETABLE STOCK

3 ONIONS, INCLUDING SKINS,
   ROUGHLY CHOPPED
3 LEEKS, ROUGHLY CHOPPED
3 CARROTS, ROUGHLY CHOPPED
2 STICKS OF CELERY, ROUGHLY
   CHOPPED
1 FENNEL BULB, ROUGHLY CHOPPED
225 G/8 OZ TOMATOES, ROUGHLY
   CHOPPED

**MAKES ABOUT 1.5 LITRES/
2½ PINTS**
Place all the ingredients except the
tomatoes in a large saucepan. Add
1.5 litres/2½ pints cold water.
Bring slowly to the boil, then
simmer for 1 hour.

   Add the tomatoes and cook for
a further 30 minutes. Strain and
season to taste.

THE MASTER CHEFS

SOUPS
ARABELLA BOXER

MEZE, TAPAS AND ANTIPASTI
AGLAIA KREMEZI

PASTA SAUCES
GORDON RAMSAY

RISOTTO
MICHELE SCICOLONE

SALADS
CLARE CONNERY

MEDITERRANEAN
ANTONY WORRALL THOMPSON

VEGETABLES
PAUL GAYLER

LUNCHES
ALASTAIR LITTLE

COOKING FOR TWO
RICHARD OLNEY

FISH
RICK STEIN

CHICKEN
BRUNO LOUBET

SUPPERS
VALENTINA HARRIS

THE MAIN COURSE
ROGER VERGÉ

ROASTS
JANEEN SARLIN

WILD FOOD
ROWLEY LEIGH

PACIFIC
JILL DUPLEIX

CURRIES
PAT CHAPMAN

HOT AND SPICY
PAUL AND JEANNE RANKIN

THAI
JACKI PASSMORE

CHINESE
YAN-KIT SO

VEGETARIAN
KAREN LEE

DESSERTS
MICHEL ROUX

CAKES
CAROLE WALTER

COOKIES
ELINOR KLIVANS

THE MASTER·CHEFS

This edition produced for The Book People Ltd,

Hall Wood Avenue, Haydock, St Helens WA11 9UL

Text © copyright 1996 Valentina Harris

Valentina Harris has asserted her right to be
identified as the Author of this Work.

Photographs © copyright 1996 Simon Wheeler

First published in 1996 by
WEIDENFELD & NICOLSON
THE ORION PUBLISHING GROUP
ORION HOUSE
5 UPPER ST MARTIN'S LANE
LONDON WC2H 9EA

British Library Cataloguing-in-Publication data
A catalogue record for this book is available
from the British Library.

ISBN 0 297 83637 4

DESIGNED BY THE SENATE
EDITOR MAGGIE RAMSAY
FOOD STYLIST JOY DAVIES
ASSISTANT KATY HOLDER